Climbing Orangutans

by Shannon Knudsen

PULL AHEAD BOOKS
Animals

Lerner Publications Company • Minneapolis

Lerner Publications Company
A division of Lerner Publishing Group, Inc.
241 First Avenue North
Minneapolis, MN 55401 U.S.A.

Website address: www.lernerbooks.com

Words in *italic* type are explained in a glossary on page 30.

Library of Congress Cataloging-in-Publication Data

Knudsen, Shannon, 1971–
    Climbing orangutans / by Shannon Knudsen.
        p.   cm. — (Pull ahead books)
    ISBN-13: 978-0-8225-6704-2 (lib. bdg. : alk. paper)
    ISBN-10: 0-8225-6704-0 (lib. bdg. : alk. paper)
    1. Orangutan—Juvenile literature. I. Title.
    QL737.P96K58 2008
    599.88'3—dc22   2006024167

Manufactured in the United States of America
1 2 3 4 5 6 — JR — 13 12 11 10 09 08

J
599.88
Knu
7/07

This animal has climbed very high. What kind of animal is this?

This animal is an orangutan.

Orangutans live in *rain forests*.
Rain forests are full of trees.

An orangutan spends most of its time in trees. It eats in trees.

It drinks
water in
trees.

It even rests in trees.

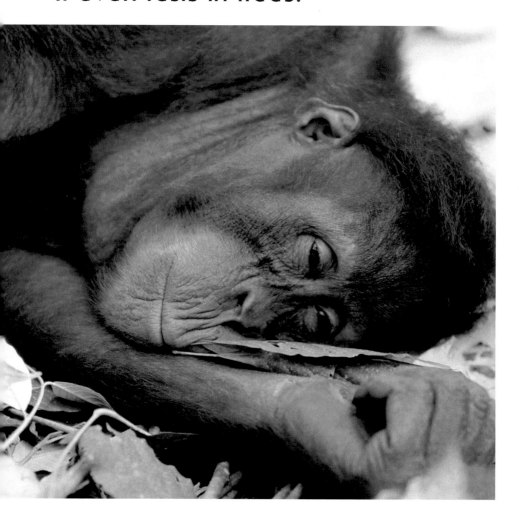

Why do orangutans spend so much time in trees?

The trees are full of food.

Orangutans are *omnivores*.
Omnivores eat plants and animals.
Orangutans eat mostly fruit.

They also eat leaves, bark, and insects. Sometimes they catch small lizards too.

Trees are safe places for orangutans.
It is hard for animals that hunt
orangutans to catch them in tall trees.

Orangutans are very good at climbing trees. They have long, strong arms.

Orangutans grip branches with their hands and feet. Fingers, thumbs, and toes bend. They hold on tight.

An orangutan has fingernails. It has toenails on its toes.

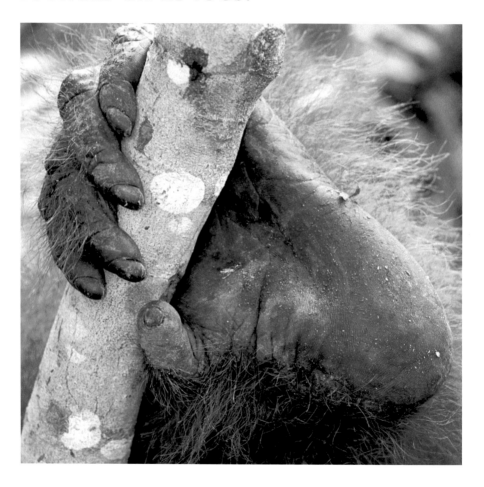

Hands and feet help an orangutan move from tree to tree. The orangutan climbs and swings from branch to branch.

Hands also
help grab
food.

What else
can an
orangutan
do with its
hands?

An orangutan can build nests. The
nests are made of branches and
leaves. Orangutans sleep in nests.

An orangutan also holds tools
in its hands. This orangutan is
holding a stick.

Mother orangutans use their hands
to hold their young. What is a very
young orangutan called?

A very young orangutan
is called a *baby*.

Young orangutans drink milk from their mother. This is called *nursing*.

The mother orangutan teaches
her baby. The baby learns to find
food and build a nest. It learns to
climb too.

Baby orangutans grow slowly.
They stay with their mothers until
they are seven years old.

By then, an orangutan is no longer
a baby.

It is very good at climbing! It can
take care of itself.

ASIA

Sumatra

Borneo

INDONESIA

KEY:

■ shows where orangutans live

This is a map of Indonesia.
Where do orangutans live?

Parts of an Orangutan's Body

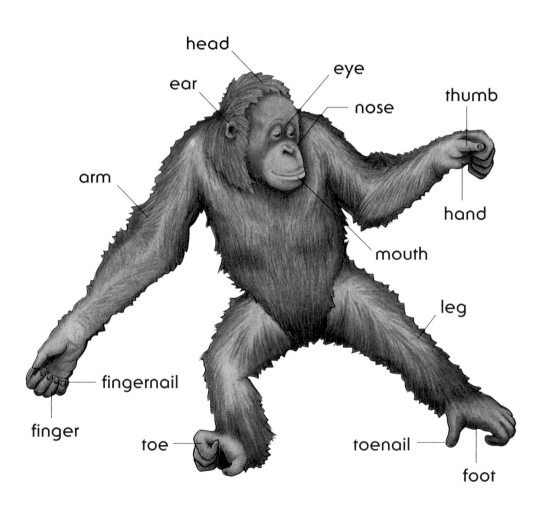

head

eye

ear

thumb

nose

arm

hand

mouth

leg

fingernail

finger

toe

toenail

foot

Glossary

baby: a very young orangutan

nursing: drinking milk from a mother's body

omnivores: animals that eat both plants and animals

rain forests: forests where heavy rain falls frequently

Further Reading and Websites

Eckert, Edana. *Orangutan*. New York: Children's Press, 2003.

Kendall, Patricia. *Orangutans*. Chicago: Raintree, 2004.

Animalplanet.com
http://animal.discovery.com/fansites/janegoodall/
interactives/greatape/greatape.html
This site provides basic information about orangutans and a video of orangutans making and using tools and solving problems.

Creature Feature: Orangutans
http://www.nationalgeographic.com/kids/creature
_feature/0102/orangutans.html
Learn fun facts about orangutans on the National
Geographic.com Kids site. On this site, visitors can
use interactive features, watch a video, hear the
sounds orangutans make, view a map to see where
they live, and send an electronic postcard to a friend.

Orangutans: Just Hangin' On
http://www.pbs.org/wnet/nature/orangutans
This site offers lots of photos and information, a map,
resources to contact, and additional links to learn
more about orangutans.

Index

Photo Acknowledgments

The photographs in this book are used with the permission of: © PhotoDisc Royalty Free by Getty Images, p. 3; © Timothy G. Laman/National Geographic/Getty Images, p. 4; © Brian Rogers/Visuals Unlimited, p. 5; © age fotostock/SuperStock, pp. 6, 8, 15; © Frans Lanting/Minden Pictures, p. 7; © Theo Allofs/Visuals Unlimited, pp. 9, 16, 17, 22, 23, 26; © Ralph Clevenger/Corbis, p. 10; © Getty Images, pp. 11, 13; © Ingo Arndt/naturepl.com, p. 12; © Michael K. Nichols/National Geographic/Getty Images, p. 14; © Nick Garbutt/naturepl.com, p. 18; © Shane Moore/Animals Animals, p. 19; © Anup Shah/naturepl.com, pp. 20, 24, 25; © Hope Ryden/National Geographic/Getty Images, p. 21; © Co Rentmeester/Time & Life Pictures/Getty Images, p. 27.

Front cover: © Theo Allofs/Visuals Unlimited